QUESTIONS AND ANSWERS
ABOUT
SCIENCE

Capella

This edition published in 2008 by Arcturus Publishing Limited,
26/27 Bickels Yard, 151-153 Bermondsey Street,
London SE1 3HA

Copyright © 2008 Arcturus Publishing Limited

ISBN 978-1-84837-160-6

Designers: Q2A India and Jane Hawkins
Editors: Ella Fern, Fiona Tulloch and Alex Woolf

Printed in China

Contents

Introduction   7
Origin of Life   8
Matter   10
Light   12
Sound   14
Heat   16
Electricity   18
Magnets   20
Forces and Motion   22
Land Transport   24
Water Transport   26
Air Transport   28
Index   30

Introduction

Our knowledge and understanding of the physical world is advancing all the time. Through the painstaking work of generations of scientists we have managed to solve many of the mysteries of the universe, and even develop theories about the origin of life. We understand how a rainbow forms, what an echo is and why an icecube melts. We can calculate the forces at work when a racing car accelerates or a bungee jumper leaps from a bridge. Scientists and engineers have put this knowledge to practical use in the technology we see all around us, from lightbulbs and magnetic compasses to supersonic jet aircraft.

As you read, you will discover many fascinating facts about the world of science. For example, what is a super atom? Why is the sky blue? How does a light bulb work? And what is the land speed record? You will find the answers to these and many other questions in the pages of this book.

Origin of Life

The Earth was formed about 4.5 billion years ago. But the earliest fossils found show that life on Earth only began about 3.5 billion years ago.

▼ Early Earth
Artist's impression of how the Earth looked in the early days—mostly water, a few volcanic islands, and dinosaurs roaming the land, seas and sky.

Quick Q's:

1. Why is the coelacanth called a living fossil?

The coelacanth is one of the earliest known fish that has survived until today. It grows to a length of 2 meters (6.5 feeet). Until a coelacanth was caught by a fisherman off the east coast of South Africa in 1938, it was thought to be extinct.

2. What are the different ages in which life formed?

Life began in the Precambrian age. Then came the Palaeozoic age, which saw the first plants, most invertebrates, the first vertebrates, fish, amphibians, and reptiles. The Mesozoic age or the Age of Reptiles was when dinosaurs ruled the Earth. This was also when flowering plants, birds, and some mammals developed. Humans only appeared much later, in the Cenozoic period.

3. Is there any new clue on how life began?

Scientists have found some animals among the mixture of gases that come out of volcanoes. Much of Earth was like this when life began. So any animal that can live here may hold a clue to the origin of life on Earth.

Q What was the Earth like in the early days?

A When the Earth began, it was hot, dry and dusty. There was no oxygen. According to some scientists, the blue-green algae were the first living things to appear. They produced their own food and oxygen using sunlight—a process called photosynthesis that plants use today. Slowly, the oxygen in the atmosphere increased, and larger organisms were able to develop.

Q Did life definitely start on Earth?

A Some scientists believe life didn't begin on Earth, but came from outer space. They believe that a comet hit the Earth, carrying the proteins from which living things are formed. There are a number of theories regarding the origin of life on Earth (or in space), but none of them have been proven yet.

Q When did the first animals appear?

A Between about 600 million years ago and 517 million years ago, the first animals appeared in the oceans. They had soft bodies. These flat creatures were the ancestors of sea anemones, sea urchins, jellyfish and worms. They were all invertebrates—animals without a spine.

▶ First spine
Artist's impression of how the Pikaia probably looked. This seahorse lookalike is important as it was the very first vertebrate.

Q What was the first animal with a spine?

A The first animal with a spine was called the pikaia. It looked like a flat worm and was about 5 centimeters (2 inches) long. It swam close to the sea floor, by twisting its body back and forth and using its tail fin to steer. The pikaia is now extinct.

Q When did the first fish appear?

A The pikaia was followed by fish without jaws, so their mouths had to remain open to catch plants and animals as they swam by. Then, about 475 million years ago, the coelacanth developed jaws and teeth. Since they could eat more effectively, these fish with jaws grew faster. Amazingly, coelacanths are still around today!

Studying those that died ages ago

Scientists called paleontologists study the lives of prehistoric plants and animals by looking at fossils. When these animals and plants died, soil settled on top of them. Over time, this soil gradually hardened into rock. This happened again and again till there were several layers of rock, with the oldest layer at the bottom. The print of the dead animal or plant that died during a certain period can be seen clearly on the rocks. These prints are called fossils. Fossils have helped us to discover what life was like before humans were around.

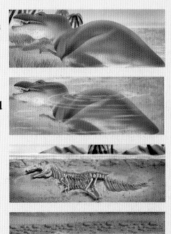

Q When did the first land creatures appear?

A As the seas filled with more animals feeding on one another, some marine creatures (including some fish) began to move to land to escape their predators and to get food more easily. Some of these creatures developed into insects like mayflies and dragonflies. They grew lungs and their fins changed to legs. These were the very first amphibians—animals that could live either on land or in water. A typical animal of this period was the acanthostega. It had four stubby feet and looked like a lizard. It spent most of its time on the shores of lagoons.

▼ Ancestor of amphibians
This armored fish may have been the ancestor of amphibians who first left the sea and started to move on to land. Fins below the body may be the precursor to legs.

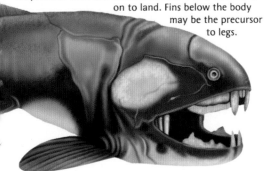

▼ Clues to early forms of life
Stromatolites are stone structures that may have been formed by organisms such as the blue-green algae, when they cemented the sediments at the bottom of the sea. Scientists have found fossilized remains of some very early life inside stromatolites.

Matter

Everything around us is matter. Anything that occupies space and has weight is matter. Matter is made up of atoms and molecules. It takes three main forms: solid, liquid and gas. All matter can change from one of these forms to another.

Q What does matter look like?

A Matter is found in different forms and shapes. It can be as huge as a mountain or as tiny as gravel. It can be hard like diamond, or as soft as silk. Even water is matter. A cube of ice is the solid state of water. At the melting point of water, or a little over 0 °C, the ice turns into water. If the water is boiled, it turns into steam or gas. When this steam meets a cold surface, like a tile on the kitchen wall, it cools and becomes liquid. Plasma, another form of matter, can be made from a gas.

◄ **Underground water**
A geyser blows steam into the cold air of Iceland. The temperature underground can be so high that the water turns into steam. This steam then expands and looks for ways out of its chamber. When it finds a pipe leading to a hole on the Earth's surface, it gushes out in the form of a geyser. On contact with the cold air outside, the steam cools down and turns back to water again.

Q What are solids?

A Anything that has a shape of its own and occupies space or has volume is a solid. An ice cube is a solid. When it melts into water, it turns into a liquid that has volume but no definite shape. If you pour the liquid into a spoon, it takes the shape of the spoon. If you pour it back into the ice tray, it takes the shape of the ice tray. If the water is heated to a certain temperature, it becomes vapor or gas and has no definite shape or volume. Gas expands to fill any container you put it into.

▼ **Crystal of carbon atoms**
A diamond is a transparent crystal of carbon atoms. It is one of the many forms in which carbon is found.

▲ **All three forms**
The ice cubes (top), the water in a cup (top right) and the vapor in front of the kettle (above) are the three forms in which water can be found—solid, liquid and gas. All three forms are interchangeable, by adding or taking heat energy away from the water. The chemical properties of water remain the same in all states.

Q What is matter made of?

A The tiniest part of all matter is an atom. Several atoms form a molecule. Matter in solid state, like the ice cube, gets its shape because the atoms are packed close and tight. In the liquid state, atoms are more loosely packed. In the gas state, the atoms are even more spread out and have lots of space between them.

Q How does an ice cube become water?

A Adding more energy or taking away energy from a substance changes its form. When you add heat energy to an ice cube, it turns to water. This is a physical change since its shape and state change but the chemical composition, or the atoms and molecules, do not change.

Tiny orbit

Atoms are made up of three parts called electrons, neutrons and protons. The neutrons and protons form the nucleus, or center, of the atom and the electrons move around the nucleus. An electron has a negative electric charge, the proton has a positive electric charge and the neutron is neutral or has no charge. The atomic theory was first developed by John Dalton (below).

Q What are chemical changes?

A Sometimes, adding or taking away energy changes the substance so much that no amount of heating or cooling can turn it back to what it was. This is called a chemical change. When you heat or toast bread, it turns brown and finally gets burned or black. No amount of cooling can turn this brown bread white again because the bread has been through a chemical change.

Q What is a compound?

A All matter is made up of some basic substances called elements. Elements are natural substances. They cannot be made artificially. Oxygen is an element. If two or more elements are combined in such a way that they can be separated again, it is called a mixture. When you combine two or more elements to make something new that cannot be changed, you get a compound. If you heat iron and sulphur, it will form iron sulphide, which is a compound.

◄ Different shapes
A liquid does not have a specific shape but takes the shape of the container in which it is poured. This is because the atoms that make up the liquid are freer than they are in solid form, so they move about more and occupy all the space.

▲ A chemical change
When you toast a slice of bread, it is a chemical change. The heat leads to chemical reactions in the bread, so that it hardens and changes color.

Try these too...

Light (12–13), Sound (14–15), Heat (16–17), Electricity (18–19), Magnets (20–21), Forces and Motion (22–23)

◄ Plasma
This is matter in its plasma state, the fourth state of matter. When gases become very hot, like in these neon tubes, they turn into plasma and start glowing. In this state, electrons and protons move about freely, so that the matter is said to be ionized. Neon lighting is used widely in cities.

Light

Light is a very important part of our lives. Without light we would not be able to see the beautiful world around us, and it wouldn't even exist. Light is essential for life to thrive on this planet. Animals and humans depend on plants for their food. Plants make their own food, but they cannot do so without light.

Quick Q's:

1. What is a light year?

The distance that light travels in a year is called a light year.

2. What color is light?

Light usually appears white, but is made up of various colors of the rainbow: red, orange, yellow, green, blue, indigo, and violet (ROYGBIV).

3. Why does the Sun look like a red disc during sunrise and sunset?

During sunrise and sunset, the sunlight has to travel a much longer distance than during the rest of the day. The scattered blue light is not able to cover this extra distance and therefore does not reach our eyes. The red light reaches us, as the wavelength of red is longer. This helps red light travel further. This is why the Sun appears like a red disc.

4. What do the words "opaque" and "transparent" mean?

Solids are said to be opaque, as they do not allow light to pass through them, while water and glass are transparent as light is able to pass through.

Q **How long does it take for sunlight to travel to the Earth?**

A Light from the Sun takes about eight minutes to reach us on the Earth. This is because sunlight travels at an incredible speed of about 300,000 kilometers per second (186,000 miles per second). Nothing in this universe travels faster than that!

▲ **Source of light**
Light is actually a form of energy that is produced by both natural and artificial sources. A light source is any object that gives off light. The Sun is the main natural source of light. Artificial sources of light include candles and electric bulbs.

Q **Does light always travel in a straight line?**

A Light travels in a straight line unless an object is placed in its path. If the object is solid the light bends around the edges of the object, creating a shadow. If you place a mirror in its path, the light hits the surface and gets reflected. If you use a transparent object, the light goes through it, but its direction is altered slightly. This phenomenon is called refraction.

Q **Why are we not able to see objects on the other side of a wall?**

A We are able to see an object when light bounces off that object and reaches our eyes. However, solid objects like a wall block the light from passing through to the other side. Instead, the light hits the wall and bounces back. Therefore, we are able to see the wall but not the objects on the other side.

◀ **A matter of color**
The color of an object is determined by the color of the light it scatters—an object appears green because it scatters green and absorbs the rest of the colors. A black object is black because it does not scatter any light.

Q Glass is also a solid object, yet how are we able to see through it?

A The molecules of solid matter are usually packed tightly together, and therefore do not allow light to pass through them. In liquids and gases, the molecules move about freely and there is a lot of space between them. That is why light is able to pass through these materials easily. Glass is made by first melting sand, and then cooling it. The substance made has the rigidity of a solid, but still has the free moving molecules of a liquid. So the space between the molecules of glass allows light to pass through, although glass itself is a solid.

Q How are rainbows formed?

A A rainbow is created by the refraction of sunlight by water droplets in the atmosphere. When sunlight passes through a drop of water, it is bent in such a way that the various colors that make up white light are split. Each color is bent at different angles. Red bends the least, while violet is bent the most. It is this phenomenon that we see as a rainbow.

▼ A rainbow of colors
The rainbow is always formed on that portion of the sky that is directly opposite to the Sun. A rainbow is not composed of just seven colors. In fact, it also contains colors like infrared that cannot be seen.

Mirror, mirror!

Light usually bounces straight back when it hits a solid object. We can see the object, but it doesn't reflect anything. However, some objects also absorb a part of the light that falls on them and reflect it. Others reflect all of the light that falls on them. These objects create reflections. Reflections are seen best on mirrors as they have smooth, flat surfaces that reflect light better. When you stand in front of a mirror, the reflected light from it falls on you and therefore you are able to see an image of yourself on the mirror.

Q Why is the sky blue?

A The Earth's atmosphere contains tiny molecules of gas and dust particles. Sunlight entering the atmosphere hits these molecules and dust particles. Colors with longer wavelengths, like red and yellow, can pass through the atmosphere without being scattered by these molecules of gas and dust particles. But the color blue, with its shorter wavelength, is scattered by the gas molecules and the dust in the upper atmosphere. This is why the sky appears blue.

▶ Blue water
Water is actually colorless. However, large amounts of water act like the sky and scatter blue light. This is why seas, lakes and rivers usually appear blue.

Try these too...

Matter (10–11), Sound (14–15), Heat (16–17), Electricity (18–19), Magnets (20–21), Forces and Motion (22–23)

Sound

Sound is a form of energy that is transferred by pressure waves in air or through other materials. These waves can be picked up by the ear, which is how we hear sounds. But there are many sounds around us that our ears do not pick up, and so we do not hear them.

Quick Q's:

1. What is the range of sound that the human ear can catch?

A young human being can hear almost all sounds from 15 Hz to 20,000 Hz. With age, you hear less, and find it difficult to catch higher frequencies. A human voice carries sound at about 60 Hz, but a shout can reach 13,000 Hz. Elephants, dogs and other animals can hear ultrasonic sound that we cannot.

2. How does ultrasonic sound help doctors?

Ultrasonic sound waves help doctors locate and diagnose medical problems, because different tissues reflect sound waves in different ways. Using this method, doctors can also monitor the development of a fetus during pregnancy.

3. How do I speak?

Human beings have vocal chords inside the larynx which produce sound. When air passes through a gap between the chords, these chords vibrate and produce a sound. All animals that can produce a sound have vocal chords, except birds which produce sound through a bony ring, called a syrinx.

Q How does sound move?

A Sound needs a medium like air, water or solids to travel through. When something moves through the air, it disturbs the molecules of gas in the air around it. The air vibrates or moves back and forth. This vibration is heard as sound. The greater the vibration, the louder the sound. Since sound travels in waves, it gets weaker the further it travels. That is why your voice cannot be heard beyond a certain distance. If you put in more energy and shout, the sound waves will be stronger and travel further so that your voice can be heard further. Sound cannot travel through a vacuum, because a vacuum is completely empty, and has no medium with which to carry the sound wave.

Q Can you measure sound?

A Sound is measured in several ways: frequency, wavelength and amplitude. Sound waves vibrate at different rates. These are called frequencies, measured in cycles per second or Hertz (Hz). 1 Hertz = 1 vibration per second. A wavelength measures the length of one cycle. Longer wavelengths have a lower pitch. The lowest tones that a human can catch are about 16 vibrations per second, or 16 Hz. Amplitude measures how loud the sound is. A sound wave of high amplitude will produce a louder sound. It is measured in decibels (Db).

◄ Music to the ears
Music generally conforms to eight notes or an octave. All other sound is noise. Although most of us agree on what music is, there can be disagreements. For example, people beating on pots and pans can create unusual music.

Q Does sound travel as fast as light?

A Sound travels far slower than light. Light travels at 299,337 kilometers per second, (186,000 miles per second) and sound travels at about 340 meters per second (1,116 feet per second). This is why we see lightning before we hear thunder. If you hear a clap of thunder ten seconds after you see a flash of lightning, then the lightning struck 3.6 kilometers (two miles) away.

Q What is an echo?

A Sound waves can be reflected off any reasonably flat surface like a cliff, high wall or mountain. When this surface is neither too near nor too far, a sound made by you hits the surface and comes back to you as an echo. The further the surface is from you, the weaker the echo and the longer it will take for the echo to return. The waves keep bouncing back and forth, getting weaker as they travel, until they lose energy and die out.

▼ **Sonic boom**
When an aircraft flies faster than the speed of sound, it is hitting the sound waves in front before those waves have moved away. So successive sound waves are getting mixed up. This creates the sonic boom.

How the ear hears

When sound energy reaches the outer ear, the eardrum that separates the outer and middle ears transmits this sound inside, where it is converted into nerve signals and sent to the brain. The brain tells us what we hear. We hear our own voice much the way we hear other sounds, and also by bone conduction. The vibration of the voice makes the bones in our skull vibrate. These vibrations are picked up by the inner ear. That is how some people with hearing problems can be helped with a hearing aid that transfers sound vibrations to the skull bones.

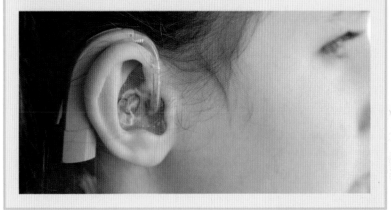

Q How does an aircraft break the sound barrier?

A Supersonic aircraft travel at a speed greater than that of the speed of sound, which is about 1,224 kilometers per hour (765 miles per hour). The first supersonic flight was in 1947 by a Bell X-1 rocket plane flown by Chuck Yeager. These aircraft measure speed in Mach. Mach 1 is the speed of sound. At less than Mach 1, the aircraft is flying at a speed lower than the speed of sound or is subsonic. At Mach 1, it is traveling at the speed of sound or is transonic. Speed between Mach 1 to 5 is supersonic. Above Mach 5 is hypersonic. At supersonic speed and above, an aircraft creates such a strong shock wave that it is heard on the ground as a sonic boom. This can be so loud that most supersonic aircraft fly above Mach 1 only above the ocean, where few people outside will be troubled by the sonic boom.

Try these too...

Matter (10–11), Light (12–13), Heat (16–17), Electricity (18–19), Magnets (20–21), Forces and Motion (22–23), Air Transport (28–29)

▲ **Sharp ears**
Dogs can pick up a lower frequency than humans can. Dog whistles are made on this principle.

Heat

Heat is a form of energy that is created by atoms moving. Even things that are cold have some heat energy because their atoms move, albeit slowly. When we feel cold, we jump up and down for warmth to get our atoms moving! Heat energy is also known as thermal energy. Many types of energy like light, chemical, sound and nuclear can be converted into heat energy by increasing the speed of the atoms in the object producing the energy.

Quick Q's:

1. What is thermodynamics?

Thermodynamics is the study of heat and how it can help us.

2. Why do things expand when heated?

When you heat solids, liquids or gases, they expand because the molecules start moving faster. To move fast, they need more space, so they expand.

3. What is boiling point?

The temperature at which a substance changes from liquid to gas is called its boiling point. The melting point of a substance is the temperature at which it changes from solid to liquid.

4. What are good conductors of heat?

Metals are the best conductors of heat. That is why cooking pans are made of metal to carry the heat from the stove to the pan. Wood and plastic are poor conductors. That is why the handles of cooking utensils are often made of these materials, so we don't burn our hands!

Q Where do we find heat?

A
The largest source of heat in nature is the Sun. The Sun is a burning ball of fire whose average surface temperature is 6,000 °C (10,800 °F) about 400 times the average surface temperature on Earth. In the kitchen, we need heat to convert raw food into something that is digested easily. We use gas or an electric oven to heat our food. Before stoves, heaters and ovens running on gas or electricity were developed, the heat for cooking was provided by burning wood or coal. Vehicles like cars move with the heat that comes from burning fossil fuels like petroleum and diesel. Machines like a knife sharpener or an electrical saw generate heat. Our bodies get heat energy from the food we eat. But ultimately, the source of all this heat is the Sun. Even the fires that burn under the Earth's crust produce heat that originally came from the Sun.

◀ From heat to light
The heat energy produced by the burning of the matchstick also produces visible light. The lighted match is used to light the wick of the candle. As the wick catches fire, it produces heat. Some of this heat energy is converted into light energy that we see. Another portion of the heat energy melts the wax to provide fuel, so that the entire process can continue.

Q How is heat measured?

A
Heat is measured with a thermometer. A thermometer is a glass tube that ends in a bulb containing mercury. Numbers are written on the tube. The mercury in the bulb heats up when it touches something hot, like the inside of your mouth. As a result, the mercury expands and rises up the tube. If we do not have a fever and are resting, the mercury will stop at 37.0 °C (98.6 °F). When we are unwell and have a fever, the mercury rises further, and the doctor knows how high the fever is.

Q What is heat energy used for?

A
We use heat energy every day. Electrical energy is converted into heat energy in appliances like electrical stoves, toasters, hair dryers and light bulbs. When you boil water, heat energy from the stove makes the molecules in the pan move faster. This heats up the pan. This heat from the pan, in turn, makes water molecules inside it move faster and heat up. That is why the water heats up only after the pan is hot. Heat energy does a lot of work for us. The earliest trains ran on thermal power from burning coal.

◀ Using heat
One of the most common uses of heat energy is for cooking food. The heat leads to chemical changes, which turns raw food into cooked food that we can digest.

Q How is heat transferred from one thing to another?

A Heat is transferred by conduction, convection and radiation. Conduction means the transfer of energy from one molecule to the next molecule. Whenever two substances come close to each other, heat flows from the warmer to the cooler substance through conduction. Convection is when a source of heat warms up a liquid or gas due to movements of currents inside the liquid or gas. This is how water boils. Radiation is the transfer of heat in straight lines like the rays of the Sun. Direct radiation from the Sun can be dangerous because it contains ultraviolet rays that damage our skin.

Q How can I light a fire?

A When two things rub against each other, it is called friction. This generates a lot of heat, sometimes enough heat to light a fire without matches. People struck pieces of flint to light a fire before matches were developed. Even today, when you light a match, it is friction that causes the matchstick to catch fire.

▼ Transfer of heat in a microwave oven
Microwave radiation passes through the food inside this oven. Some molecules in the food absorb energy from the microwave beam and start moving around. This movement produces heat that cooks the food.

The largest source of heat energy

Heat energy from the Sun is known as solar energy. Rays from the Sun heat the surface of the Earth, the oceans and the air above. Taking a hint from the Sun's natural heating capacity, scientists have made solar cells from which we can get electricity. When sunlight touches a solar cell, it causes a chemical reaction and electricity is generated. Solar panels can heat water and cook food and solar cells can even run a car. Fossils fuels like petroleum have to be mined from the Earth, and one day we will use them all up. But solar power will not run out for millions of years.

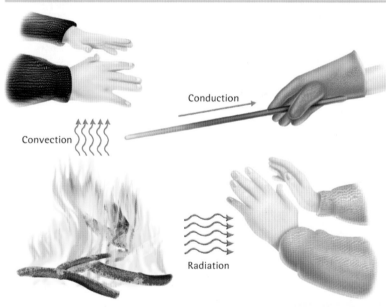

Convection

Conduction

Radiation

▲ Ways of heat transfer
Heat travels through solids by conduction. Most metals are good conductors of heat, while wood is a poor conductor. That is why frying pans are made of metal, but often have a wooden handle. As the diagram shows, convection currents first move upward. Heat transfer by radiation takes place in all directions.

Try these too...

Matter (10–11), Light (12–13), Electricity (18–19), Forces and Motion (22–23)

Electricity

Electricity is a secondary source of energy. We have to generate electricity from primary sources of energy like moving water, nuclear power, coal or natural gas. It can be converted into other forms of energy like light or heat. Electricity is used for lighting and heating or cooling our homes. It runs machines to wash clothes and dishes and to cook. It brings us information through computers and television.

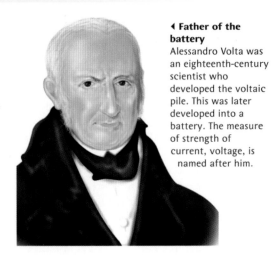

◄ Father of the battery
Alessandro Volta was an eighteenth-century scientist who developed the voltaic pile. This was later developed into a battery. The measure of strength of current, voltage, is named after him.

▲ Electric animal
One of the large electric eels of South America can deliver a shock powerful enough to kill a human.

Quick Q's:

1. If electricity lights a bulb, does it also light my torch?

A bulb is lit with electricity from a power generator. Another source of electricity is the battery. It has chemicals that react and produce a small amount of electricity, enough for a torch.

2. How do power stations generate so much electricity?

Power stations convert the kinetic energy of moving water (hydroelectricity), heat produced by burning coal (thermal electricity) or by a nuclear reaction (nuclear power), the kinetic energy of wind that turns a windmill, tide movements (tidal power) or heat from inside the Earth (geothermal power) to generate electricity.

Q Who discovered electricity?

A Ancient Greeks knew that electricity could be produced by rubbing two pieces of felt together. But the first use of the word electricity was by Sir Thomas Browne in his 1646 book *Pseudodoxia Epidemica* (Vulgar Errors). In 1752, Benjamin Franklin proved that lightning was created by electric charges. He tied an iron key to a kite string during a storm and showed that the lightning hit the key. For this reason, Franklin is said to have discovered electricity. Today, we know that lightning is the most commonly seen form of natural electricity. It is caused by clouds carrying a negative charge that bump into positively charged objects on Earth.

Q What is electricity?

A Everything is made of atoms. At the center of an atom is the nucleus made of protons and neutrons. An atom also has tiny electrons which spin around the nucleus. Electrons have a negative electrical charge, and protons have a positive charge. The electrons don't stay in one place. They move around to different atoms, so some atoms have more protons, some have more electrons. An atom with more protons is positively charged. One with more electrons is negatively charged. When the electrons pass from one atom to the next, it creates an electric current.

Q Can electricity make my hair stand on end ?

A Static electricity is created when you rub against a charged surface. The extra electrons move from your body or the other way around, and a tiny spark of electricity is created. Static makes dry hair stand on end after you run a plastic comb through it.

◄ Natural electricity
The lightning that transfers electrons from negatively charged clouds to positively charged substances on the surface of the Earth is the biggest source of natural electricity we know of. Lightning can be dangerous to someone caught outdoors. Anyone caught outdoors during a thunderstorm should keep as low as possible.

Q How is electricity measured?

A Voltage is the measure of the strength of an electric current. The unit for measuring voltage is the volt. A voltameter tells us how many electrons are sent from one end of the circuit and how many are received at the other end. The distance electricity travels affects its quality, especially if it is prevented from flowing freely because of resistance. Resistance is a material's opposition to the flow of electric current through it. Resistance is measured in ohms. Scientists are always looking for materials like copper that are good conductors of electricity and have a low resistance. Silver is the best conductor, but it cannot be used in wires in our homes because it is too costly. Most metals are good conductors.

Q How does a light bulb work?

A The electric bulb is made of transparent or translucent glass and has a delicate wire called a filament. It has to be thin so that its atoms collide more often when an electric current is passed through it. That is how it glows. Thomas Alva Edison made the first practical, workable bulb for home use. Compact fluorescent lamps that use less energy than other bulbs have become increasingly popular since the 1980s.

▶ **Inside a bulb**
Scientists experimented with the conversion of electrical energy to light throughout the nineteenth century. In 1801, Humphry Davy made platinum strips glow by passing an electric current through them. Seven different types of light bulbs were patented in that century before the first could be used at home.

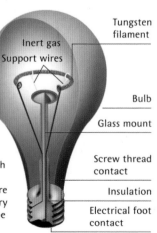

Tungsten filament
Inert gas
Support wires
Bulb
Glass mount
Screw thread contact
Insulation
Electrical foot contact

Electric brain

Without electricity, we wouldn't be able to feel anything! The human body has a continuous flow of electric current through our nerve cells. That is how the nerve cells convey messages to the brain, and we know that our back is hurting, or that someone is standing on our foot. In its turn, the brain uses these tiny electric currents to send commands to the rest of our body. Your hand turns the page when the brain commands it to do so.

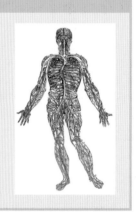

▲ **Changing skyline**
The night skyline of almost every city in the world has changed dramatically in the last 100 years or so, after electricity came into widespread use for lighting.

▼ **A hydroelectric power station**
Water is held in a dam. Then a bit of the water is allowed to run through a channel, turning the blades of a turbine connected to a generator.

Try these too...

Matter (10–11), Light (12–13), Sound (14–15), Heat (16–17), Magnets (20–21), Forces and Motion (22–23)

Magnets

Any object that attracts metals like iron, cobalt, nickel or steel to itself is a magnet. A magnet can push away or repel other magnets. Some magnets, like iron, are very strong, while other magnets are much weaker.

Quick Q's:

1. Why do things stick only to the poles of the magnet?

Magnets are strongest at their poles so objects stick to one of the poles most easily.

2. How can you destroy a magnet?

Though magnets can be natural or man-made, dropping, heating or hammering them can destroy them, especially if they are small and weak.

3. Can you store a magnet?

Magnets get weaker with time. The best way to store them is to keep them in pairs with the unlike poles next to each other and placing keepers, or pieces of soft iron, across the ends. The keepers become temporary magnets themselves and keep the magnetic force stronger.

4. What is an electromagnet?

Winding an electric wire around a piece of iron can make electromagnets. When electric current runs through the wire, a magnetic field is created. The iron piece picks this up and becomes a magnet.

Q How did people find out about magnets?

A The magnet was discovered in China as early as 200 BC. Around the same time, the Chinese found that from a magnet, one could find out directions like north and south. Sailors in most civilizations began to use a certain type of magnet called a lodestone to navigate. It is the most magnetic substance on Earth. In the sixteenth century, Sir William Gilbert discovered that a piece of iron could acquire the properties of a lodestone if you rubbed it with a lodestone. That allowed scientists to create many more magnets. People were no longer dependent on the few natural lodestones they could find. Today, magnets are made of a blend of different materials that contain some or all of iron, nickel, copper, cobalt and aluminium.

Q What are poles of a magnet?

A Just as the Earth has two poles—the North and the South Poles, a magnet also has two poles. It is easiest to find the two poles of a bar magnet where the poles at either end are equally strong. The north-seeking pole of the bar magnet points toward the Earth's North Pole. The other end points toward the South Pole. But if you use the magnet for navigation, you must remember that the magnetic poles of the Earth are not in exactly the same positions as the geographic poles of the Earth. Also, if you hold two bar magnets next to each other the poles will not point in the same direction because the magnets interfere with each other. The like poles repel each other while the unlike poles attract each other.

▲ **Magnetic scientist**
Michael Faraday (1791-1867), an English scientist, led the study of electromagnetism. He showed that magnetism could affect rays of light.

Q What is a magnetic field?

A The area around a permanent magnet has a force that can affect other magnets or magnetic materials that come near it. This area is called a magnetic field. Even the Earth has a magnetic field. It is like a huge bar magnet. Even if you cut a huge bar magnet into tiny pieces, each piece is still a magnet with its own small magnetic field.

▲ **Fridge magnets**
Most of us are familiar with the pretty and useful magnets we stick on the refrigerator.

Paper clip power

Any magnetic material in touch with a magnet starts behaving like a magnet itself. If you hang a paper clip from a magnet, it becomes a temporary magnet. You can prove it by hanging a second paper clip from the first and then another and another. However, if you remove the first clip from the magnet, all the clips below fall apart since they lose their temporary magnetism.

▶ Horseshoe magnet
You can play a variation of the paper clip game with a horseshoe magnet, which has its two poles adjacent to one another. Since the opposite poles are much closer, a horseshoe magnet produces a relatively strong magnetic field—you can stick many more clips to the magnet, starting with one that is stuck to both poles.

Q **Are mariners the only people who need magnets for their work?**

A Magnets are used almost everywhere in modern life. Most electrical appliances, from power stations to the little hair dryer at home, use a magnet to convert electrical energy into mechanical energy. Cassettes are coated with magnetic material that allows sound to be recorded on its surface. Credit cards have magnetic strips that contain encrypted information and enable us to use them. Motors found in dishwashers, fans, washing machines, refrigerators, CD, DVD and audio players use magnets. Magnets are also used to hold false teeth in place. And they help you remember too—by holding your notes to the refrigerator!

Try these too...

Matter (10–11), Light (12–13), Sound (14–15), Heat (16–17), Electricity (18–19), Forces and Motion (22–23)

This way is North

◀ The compass
Even a small pocket compass can show you the exact direction in which you are traveling. Remember that it is not the point marked North but the needle that is always pointing to the magnetic North Pole. In some compasses you can rotate the dial and align it with the needle to help you find which way is true north. The Earth's magnetic poles shift periodically. The needle points to the current pole.

Forces and Motion

Force can change the state of an object. If an object is stationary, force can get it to move. Once it is moving, force can make the object accelerate or pick up speed. It can also stop a moving object. A stationary object cannot move without force, nor can a moving object stop without force.

▲ **The discoverer of gravity**
Sir Isaac Newton (1643–1727) is supposed to have discovered gravity after seeing an apple fall from a tree.

Quick Q's:

1. What is net force?

When more than one force acts on an object, the total of all forces acting on that object is called the net force. When more than one force acts on an object in the same direction, the object moves faster. If the forces act in opposing directions, they cancel each other out to a certain extent.

2. What is lateral deflection?

It is a force that makes a bullet spin to one side, or a football curl through the air. During the Soccer World Cup in France in 1998, Brazilian Roberto Carlos scored a free kick with a perfect lateral deflection. He kicked the ball to the far right of the defenders and made it suddenly curve round and zoom into the goal.

Q Where is force used?

A Force is used in all our activities from brushing our teeth to walking, lifting and writing. Every one of our actions requires some force. You need energy to create force. Machines use force to move something or to build something.

Q What is inertia?

A An object tends to carry on doing the same thing, whether it is at rest or moving, unless a force acts on it to change that. This is called inertia. Your pencil box lies on the table until you push it. This state of rest is called inertia of rest. Then, with the force of your finger, it moves on until it meets another force that stops it. This movement is called inertia of motion. If the force you push the object with is too much, it will go beyond the point where you wanted it to go.

Q What is gravitational force?

A Gravity is the force that Sir Isaac Newton discovered, as he watched an apple fall off a tree onto the ground. It is a force that draws everything in the Earth's atmosphere and beyond toward the center of the Earth and it keeps us on the ground. Gravity does not just act on the Earth; it is the force of attraction between all bodies (things) in the universe.

◀ **The science of a kick**
The force of the kick makes the ball move. The force used by someone else's foot makes it stop.

As bodies get closer together, the force of gravity gets stronger, and as they move apart, gravity gets weaker. Bigger, heavier bodies are affected more by gravitational force. They also exert a greater force of gravity themselves. Gravity holds the solar system together and keeps the Earth close enough to the Sun for us to get the warmth we need.

Q How do I stay on a merry-go-round without flying off?

A You stay on a merry-go-round because of centripetal force. When you feel you are going to fly off into the air, it is because your body wants to keep moving in the same direction all the time. This feeling is the inertia of motion. But the centripetal force keeps attracting you to the center of the merry-go-round, making sure you stay on board! Objects set in motion normally move in a straight line because of inertia of motion, unless some other force acts upon them and changes their path. When a ball tied to a piece of string is swung round, the centripetal force acts upon the ball, attracting it to the center of the circle. The centripetal force from the string pulls the ball to keep it on its circular path.

Q What is the difference between speed and velocity?

A Speed is the distance traveled by an object in a particular time. Velocity is speed in a particular direction. Suppose you sat in a train that was moving eastward at 60 kilometers per hour (37 miles per hour). You would say that the speed of the train was 60 kilometers per hour (37 miles per hour), while its velocity was 60 kilometers per hour (37 miles per hour) east.

Q What is friction?

A Friction is a force that opposes the movement of an object by acting on it in the opposite direction. The force of friction comes into effect when two surfaces are in contact, and force is applied to make one or both of the surfaces move. Suppose you roll a ball on the floor. The ball will come to a halt after traveling a certain distance, even if it has hit nothing or no one has stopped it. The ball stops because the friction exerted by the floor acts against the motion of the ball. The soles of your new shoes probably have cuts in them to make an uneven surface.

Torque

The force that causes rotation is called torque. Torque can be measured in opening or closing a door, and it is applied when you turn a racquet from side to side. An archer applies torque to move the bow to one side when aiming an arrow. Ideally, the archer should hold the bow loose enough so that when the arrow is released, it shoots straight ahead. If the archer applies unnecessary pressure, the bow will twist upon release, the arrow will not fly straight, and the shot will miss the bull's eye.

When you run, the uneven surfaces of the shoes and the road rub against each other. This friction makes sure you do not slip while you are running. Lack of friction also causes us to slip on a wet floor since the water makes the floor smooth, which means friction is reduced. Friction produces heat. That is why when you rub a matchstick against a matchbox, sparks fly.

Try these too...

Matter (10–11), Light (12–13), Sound (14–15), Heat (16–17), Electricity (18–19), Magnets (20–21), Land Transport (24–25, Water Transport (26–27), Air Transport (28–29)

▼ **Sitting pretty**
We stay on the merry-go-around instead of flying off in one direction because of the centripetal force that holds us to its center. The force that wants to make us fly off is called the centrifugal force.

Land Transport

The earliest travel was on land. At first, people just walked. Then, they learned to tame animals for travel. They rode on horses, mules and oxen. Gradually, they made themselves more comfortable, making carts and carriages. Modern transport on land includes a wide range of vehicles such as bicycles, cars, buses and trains.

▲ **Penny farthing**
One of the early bicycle models that has gone out of use.

Quick Q's:

1. When was the first wheel invented?

As early as the fifth century BC, the Mesopotamians invented the wheel. At first it was used to make pottery but later people realized that wheels could be attached to carts and used to move things and people easily.

2. When were the first cars produced in a factory?

In 1896, thirteen Dureyas cars were made in a factory in Springfield, Massachusetts (USA). These were the very first examples of mass-produced cars.

3. What is the record speed for land travel?

The latest record speed for land travel was achieved on 15 October 1997 by Andy Green of Britain in a Thrust SSC car. He traveled at a speed of 1,233.738 kilometers per hour (766.609 miles per hour)!

▶ **Moving in luxury**
Land transport has made much progress in the twentieth century after the development and mass use of the motor car.

Q Why did early man need to travel?

A People have always needed to travel to hunt or to trade with other people. Sometimes they needed to shift home when the rains failed. At first, they tamed animals to carry them. Later, when the wheel was invented, the animals were attached to vehicles. Until recently, even human beings were used to transport others. They carried litters or sedan chairs in which the rich sat.

Q When did roads improve?

A As civilizations grew, people needed more and better roads to trade and to conquer new lands. The Romans were the first to put time and money into making all-weather roads. Rather than just smooth over a clay surface, they dug beds and filled them with crushed stone for a firm support.

The stone chips acted as a filter for rain water to flow through so the roads did not flood. On busier routes, they added paving stones to ensure that the roads were firm and dry for their chariots to move on. These roads were used to connect up the huge Roman Empire. Over time, even chariots and carts were improved with springs and shock absorbers to make the ride smoother.

Q Where were the first railroads?

A The first railroads were built in Germany around 1550. Horses pulled wagons along wooden rails and brought minerals out of mines. After the Industrial Revolution, rails were made of iron and so were the wheels. The development of the steam engine made rail transport easily available to carry people and goods over long distances.

Q When did people start to use buses?

A People traveled in stagecoaches and omnibuses pulled by horses from the early sixteenth century. The first horse-drawn tram cars came in the nineteenth century. The invention of engines that ran on steam and on fuel such as diesel and petroleum led to the development of buses as we know them.

Q When did the first cycle roll?

A In 1680, German inventor Stephan Farffler made a hand-cranked tricycle. Later, he gave it another wheel to improve its balance. In 1817, Baron Karl von Drais of Germany made the *draisiennes*, a wooden bicycle with a seat and handle bars. But since von Drais didn't think of pedals, the rider had to push with his feet on the ground. The first modern bicycle was built by Kirkpatrick Macmillan of Scotland in 1839.

Q When was the motor car made?

A The first car was designed by Nicholas Joseph Cugnot and constructed by M. Brezin in France in 1769. It ran on steam and on rails. The first non-rail automobile was made by Etienne Lenoir, also of France, in 1860. He drove the very first gas-powered car from Paris to Joinville in 1862.

▲ **Modern train**
Modern passenger trains can carry hundreds of people in comfort over all sorts of terrain.

Try these too...

Forces and Motion (22–23)

A road to drive on

Roads had to keep up with the development of technology for surface transport. McAdam designed the first highways lined with soil and stone, which is still known as macadam. The highways were higher than the land around, so that rainwater could drain off. Later, these highways were tarred and the surface was called tarmacadam or tarmac. Modern roads are built of asphalt cement or concrete.

Water Transport

The idea of traveling by water probably came to people when they watched logs and leaves float down a river. After land, water has been the second most popular medium of transportation used by humans. Early humans built simple rafts, which were improved upon in every way over thousands of years.

▲ **Galleon**
Huge sailing ships called galleons carried people and goods across the seas of the world during the Age of Exploration. The Spanish galleons were the most famous.

Quick Q's:

1. What are modern ships made of?

Boats and ships continued to be made of wood for centuries. With the start of the Industrial Revolution, people began to use steel to build ships. Today, ships are also made of aluminium and fibreglass.

2. Who was the first person to sail around the world single-handedly?

American seaman Joshua Slocum was the first man to sail around the world single-handedly. He started off from Boston on 24 April 1895, and returned to Newport, Rhode Island on 27 June 1898, having sailed 74,000 kilometers (46,000 miles) in over three years.

3. What is a hovercraft?

The hovercraft can travel on water and land. It stays suspended a few centimeters above the ground or water surface with the help of an air cushion that it creates by the thrust of its jet engines. It is used as a fast patrol boat by the police and military of several countries and also for water sports.

Q What were the first boats like?

A Rafts or planks of wood were probably the earliest modes of transportation by water. The earliest boat found dates back to 6300 BC. The boat was a hollowed-out tree trunk, also called a dugout. Some people sailed coracles, which were boats made of animal skin stretched over a wooden frame. Oars changed water transport. They allowed people to decide where they wanted to go, rather than depend on the current. Around 4000 BC, the Egyptians made long narrow boats powered by many oarsmen.

Q When were the first sails used?

A By 3000 BC, people knew how to tie a cotton sail. Sails allowed people to use wind power instead of muscle power. Now people used ships for trade. By 1200 BC, the Phoenicians and Greeks built trading ships that had special places to store the cargo. By 500 BC, they had ships with two masts.

Q How did ships navigate?

A Early ships had to sail close to shore as the sailors could not find their way in open sea. By about 100 BC, technology improved and the sailors could navigate with gadgets like the astrolabe. The early Chinese used a spoon much like a compass. Sailors from other countries also used a lodestone, which is a natural compass. By the twelfth century, the magnetic compass was in use. As the science of cartography (mapping) improved in the Middle Ages, getting lost was less of a risk for sailors. In 1757, the sextant, a device to measure latitude, was invented.

◀ **Luxury cruiser**
Modern cruise ships carry tourists in luxury and are very popular.

Q **What was special about the Viking ships?**

A By the late 1000s, the fierce Vikings of Scandinavia ruled the seas. Their famous longboats were about 24 meters (80 feet) long and 5 meters (17 feet) wide and were rowed by 40–60 oarsmen. Vikings also used small rowboats called *faering* for swift attacks on their enemies. By the twelfth century, the Vikings knew how to use a rudder to steer the ship. This gave them more control than the side steering oar. All the Viking ships were slim and fast, so they could launch deadly attacks on merchant ships and coastal areas.

Q **Was inland water travel different?**

A While sails came in handy on rivers, streams and canals required special technology to get boats on the move. Around 984 AD, the Chinese discovered how to make an inland canal lock. This connects canals at different levels and needs sound engineering skills. By 1373, Holland had a system of canal locks. On canals and rivers, boats were often drawn by horses against the flow of water, and tow-paths were made on the banks for the horses to walk on. As engineering skills improved, sometimes canals were made by tunneling under a mountain instead of going around it. Today, many canals that were earlier used for industry are tourist sites and nature reserves.

Q **How did water travel develop?**

A During the Industrial Revolution, water travel entered a new era. The development of the steam engine in the eighteenth century led to the first steamboats, which had paddle wheels to move against the current. By the late 1800s, the first iron ships came in, driven by the screw propeller. Vehicles for travel on water have now become very specialized, from the huge tankers that carry oil to luxury yachts and small speedboats.

A titanic disaster

The *Titanic* was a British luxury liner that weighed 46,000 gross tons. It was one of the grandest ships ever built, and was believed to be unsinkable. On its first voyage from Southampton to New York City, it struck an iceberg about 153 kilometers (95 miles) south of Newfoundland around midnight on 14 April 1912. It sank in less than three hours, taking about 1,513 of the 2,220 people on board with it.

Q **What are submarines?**

A A submarine is a ship that can be entirely submerged underwater. Submarines became popular during World War II since they could launch surprise attacks on enemy vessels. Early submarines had to surface often to replenish their oxygen supply. Today, submarines use nuclear power or liquid oxygen to propel their engines and can stay underwater for several months.

Q **What are ships used for today?**

A Water craft can be used for virtually any purpose now. There are car ferries and tugboats and water sports vehicles like rowing boats, kayaks, yachts and motorboats. Most big ships carry cargo from one port to another, but there are luxury ships called cruisers which carry many tourists at a time.

▲ **Rarely above water**
The sleek shape of the submarine allows it to move fast under water.

Try these too...

Forces and Motion (22–23)

Air Transport

Man has always wanted to fly. Early experiments with air travel included fancy kites, gliders and even artificial wings. Two types of aircraft can be used for air travel. Those that are lighter than air, such as hot-air balloons, and airplanes and helicopters which are heavier than air.

◀ Faster than sound
The Concorde was a commercial plane that flew faster than the speed of sound.

Quick Q's:

1. What is the Concorde?

In the 1960s, jets that could travel faster than the speed of sound were developed. These were called supersonic jets. The Concorde was a commercial supersonic jet which could fly at a height of 17,500 meters (60,000 feet) at more than twice the speed of sound.

2. What are airships?

Airships were among the earliest aircraft. They were filled with hydrogen gas or helium, which helped them to float. Engine-driven airships, called Zeppelins, were widely used by Germany in World War I to launch bombing attacks on enemy territory. Today, flexible airships are used in advertising.

3. What is a seaplane?

Seaplanes, developed by Glenn H. Curtiss, can land on and take off from the surface of water. They are useful for reaching areas where no other transport is available. There are two types of seaplanes. Floatplanes are planes with large floats instead of wheels. Flying boats are planes that float on their bellies when they land.

Q Who were the first scientists to study air travel?

A In the thirteenth century, Roger Bacon declared that he was sure air could support aircraft. At the beginning of the sixteenth century, Leonardo da Vinci studied the flight of birds and invented the propeller and the parachute. He made designs for three heavier-than-air craft, including a helicopter with a rotor that helped it rise vertically, and a glider with a wing fixed to a frame. None of these were practical at that time. But they were based on the science of flight.

◀ Joseph Michel Montgolfier
Joseph Michel and his brother Jacques Etienne Montgolfier invented the hot-air balloon. While watching wood chips rise over a fire, they realized that the burning created a gas that caued any light material over it to rise. The same principle was later used in airships.

Q What were the first aircraft like?

A Hot-air balloons were the first "aircraft." In 1783, the Montgolfier brothers successfully launched an unmanned hot-air balloon in France. The balloon was a large linen bag filled with hot air. The light, hot air carried the balloon over a distance of 2 kilometers (1.3 miles) in a flight that lasted 10 minutes. Later, with improved designs, hot-air balloons could reach a height of nearly 2,400 meters (8,000 feet) and travel a long distance.

Hydrogen-gas balloons were an improvement on the hot air balloon. Hydrogen could lift the balloon easily without being heated, as it is lighter than air. In 1785, Frenchman Pilatre de Rozier tied a helium-filled balloon and a hot-air balloon together to fly across the English Channel. Unfortunately, Rozier died when the balloons exploded.

Q Who made the first flight in a powered aircraft?

A The nineteenth century was important for the development of aviation. Sir George Cayley experimented with kites and gliders that could carry people, and he designed a helicopter. But it was not until the twentieth century that the first powered flights were made. Brothers Wilbur and Orville Wright designed and constructed an aircraft. On 17 December 1903, in North Carolina in the USA, each brother made two flights. The longest, by Wilbur, was 260 meters (852 feet) in 59 seconds. The next year, the brothers made 105 flights. One of them lasted more than five minutes. In September 1908, Orville Wright flew for more than one hour. All around the world, inventors were racing furiously to develop the first heavier-than-air plane that would fly successfully, but the Wright brothers had beaten everyone to it. Shortly after the first flight of the Wright brothers, people across the world were starting to make successful flights. In 1906 Traian Vuia made a flight in Paris and Jacob Christian Ellehammer made one in Denmark.

Q Who was the first passenger in an aircraft?

A The Wright brothers continued their research. In 1908, Orville carried the first passenger, Lieutenant Frank P. Lahm, on a flight that lasted 6 minutes and 24 seconds. Shortly afterward, Orville's plane crashed, killing another passenger, Lieutenant E. Selfridge.

Q Are aircraft used only for travel?

A Air transport is used for commercial aviation, which includes travel and ferrying cargo. It is also used by military forces to fight enemy aircraft, and for dropping bombs on enemy targets. Some aircraft are used for dusting crops with pesticides from the air, sowing clouds for rain and flying for sport.

Q What is a jet plane?

A Jet engines fly with the power from the discharge of a jet from the tail of the aircraft. They can fly at heights between 3,048 and 4,572 meters (10,000–15,000 feet). The first jet plane was flown in 1939 in Germany. Jets were used extensively during World War II to drop bombs and to fight other aircraft. Since then, jet planes have made travel by air a reality for millions of people. They can carry up to 600 passengers and fly at 680–900 kilometers per hour (420–580 miles per hour).

▼ **Aircraft carrier**
Many military planes operate out of large ships called aircraft carriers, a practice that developed in World War II.

Try these too...

Sound (14–15), Forces and Motion (22–23)

◄ **Deadly plane**
This is the famous SR-71 Blackbird of the US Air Force. The black coating of the aircraft is made out of a special material that makes it difficult to be seen by radar. At the same time, there is a special fire-control radar on the nose of the aircraft.

Strange bird

The helicopter was designed by Ján Bahyl in 1905. Helicopters are propelled by rotating overhead blades. They are slower than planes, carry fewer people and can only travel short distances. But they are an advantage in places where there is not much space, since they can land and take off vertically. They are widely used for military purposes and for rescue operations, aerial photography and fire fighting.

Index

air 14, 17
aircraft 28–29
airplanes 28, 29
airships 28
algae 8, 9
amphibians 8, 9
amplitude 14
animals 8, 9, 12, 14, 15, 24, 25, 27
atmosphere 8, 13, 22
atoms 10, 11, 16, 18, 19

batteries 18
bicycles 24, 25
boats 26–27
buses 24, 25

canal locks 27
cars 16, 17, 24, 25, 27
centrifugal force 23
centripetal force 22, 23
chemical changes 11, 16
coelecanths 8
color 12, 13
compounds 11
Concorde 28
conduction 16, 17, 19
convection 17

Dalton, John 11
diamonds 10

ears 15
Earth 8, 10, 12, 13, 16, 17, 18, 20, 21, 22
echoes 15
electric currents 18, 19, 20
electricity 10, 16, 17, 18–19
electromagnetism 20
electrons 11, 18, 19
elements 11
energy 10, 11, 12, 14, 16, 17, 18, 19, 22

Faraday, Michael 20
fish 8, 9
food 8, 12, 16, 17
forces 22–23
fossil fuels 16, 17, 18
fossils 8, 9
frequencies 14
friction 17, 23
fuel 16

gases 10, 11, 13, 14, 16, 17, 28
geothermal power 18
geysers 10
glass 13, 19
gliders 28
gravity 22

heat 10, 11, 16–17, 18, 23
helicopters 28, 29
hot-air balloons 28
hovercraft 26
human beings 8, 9, 12, 14, 15, 19, 24–29
hydroelectricity 18

ice 10, 11
inertia 22
insects 9
invertebrates 8

jet engines 26, 29
jet planes 29

kinetic electricity 18

life 8–9, 12
light 10, 12–13, 16, 18
light bulbs 12, 16, 18, 19
lightning 15, 18
liquids 10, 11, 13, 16, 17
longboats 27

magnetic compasses 21, 26
magnetic fields 20, 21
magnetic poles 20, 21

magnets 20–21
mammals 8
matter 10–11
metals 16, 17, 19, 20
microwave radiation 17
molecules 10, 11, 13, 14, 16, 17
Montgolfier brothers 28
motion 22–23
music 14

navigation 20, 21, 26
neutrons 11, 18
Newton, Sir Isaac 22
nuclear energy 16, 18, 27

oars 26
oxygen 8, 11, 27

paleontology 9
parachutes 28
photosynthesis 8
plants 8, 9, 12
plasma 10, 11
power stations 18, 19, 21
propeller 27, 28
protons 11, 18

radiation 17
railroads 25
rainbows 13
reflection 12, 13
refraction 12, 13
reptiles 8
resistance 19
roads 24, 25
rudders 27

sailing ships 26
seaplanes 28
shadows 12
ships 26–27
sky 13
solar energy 17
solids 10, 11, 12, 13, 14, 16, 17

sound 14–15, 16, 21, 28
speed 22, 23, 24, 28
static electricity 18
steam 10, 25
steam engines 25, 27
steamboats 27
submarines 27
Sun 12, 13, 16, 17, 22
sunlight 8, 12, 13
super atoms 10
supersonic aircraft 15

temperature 10, 16
thermal power 18
thermodynamics 16
thermometers 16
tidal power 18
Titanic 27
torque 23
trains 16, 24, 25
transport 24–29

ultrasonic sound 14

vaccuums 14
velocity 23
Volta, Alessandro 18
voltage 19

water 10, 11, 13, 14, 16, 17, 18, 19, 23, 26–27
wavelengths 10, 12, 13, 14
wheels 24
wind power 18, 26
Wright brothers 28, 29